I0117675

William Henry Whitmore

A Record of the Descendants of Captain John Ayres of

Brookfield, Mass.

William Henry Whitmore

A Record of the Descendants of Captain John Ayres of Brookfield, Mass.

ISBN/EAN: 9783337142094

Printed in Europe, USA, Canada, Australia, Japan

Cover: Foto ©ninafisch / pixelio.de

More available books at **www.hansebooks.com**

A

RECORD

OF

DESCENDANTS

OF

CAPTAIN JOHN AYRES,

OF

BROOKFIELD, MASS.

BY WILLIAM HENRY WHITMORE.

INTRODUCTION.

THE following pages have been prepared in the hope that such a beginning might lead to a more comprehensive record hereafter. It contains an outline of the history of a family descended from one of the worthy pioneers in the settlement of the country, a history of which the bearers of the name have so far every reason to be proud. Although from special reasons only one branch of the family has been traced with any attempt at thoroughness, this brief record presents features characteristic of New England. Our ancestor first planting on the shores of the Massachusetts Bay, was early led to seek a new home in the fertile valleys of the centre of the colony, and died a victim to the Indian hostilities which so long threatened the existence of the commonwealth. His family returned to the safer settlements on the seaboard, and descendants are still to be found along the line from Boston northward. At the revival of the settlement at Brookfield about 1717, a part of the family returned there, and from that centre has sent forth branches to Vermont, New York, Illinois, and still farther westward. In tracing the history of these

1

successive migrations then, we have an epitome of the colonization of the country. The same current has drawn off hundreds of thousands of the children of New England, until now the true New England is to be found outside of its territorial limits.

It is mainly for this reason that I have undertaken to prepare this brief history. In common with so many of the families first settled here, the Ayres family seems to be diminishing in number in Massachusetts, but to be greatly increasing, and presumably thriving, in the new States of the West. Here, however, are the records of the earlier generations, and it is a pleasant task to attempt to collect and preserve the lists, so that for the next century every one of the name may be duly cognisant of his origin.

This little pamphlet must however be regarded as but the first step. Every family should have its full history compiled, filled with those details of personal experience which are of interest to relatives and not valueless in the wider regard of the historian. It is hoped that some bearer of the name will be impelled to undertake this task before it is too late.

It remains for the compiler to thank those who have kindly assisted him by furnishing the facts here collected; and he would especially mention Ebenezer Ayres, Esq., of Cottage Grove, Minn., Rev. Rowland Ayres, of Springfield, Rev. Watson Ayres, of Neponset, and Miss Mary N. Ayres, of Medford, as having laid him under great obligations.

W. H. W.

Boston, June, 1870.

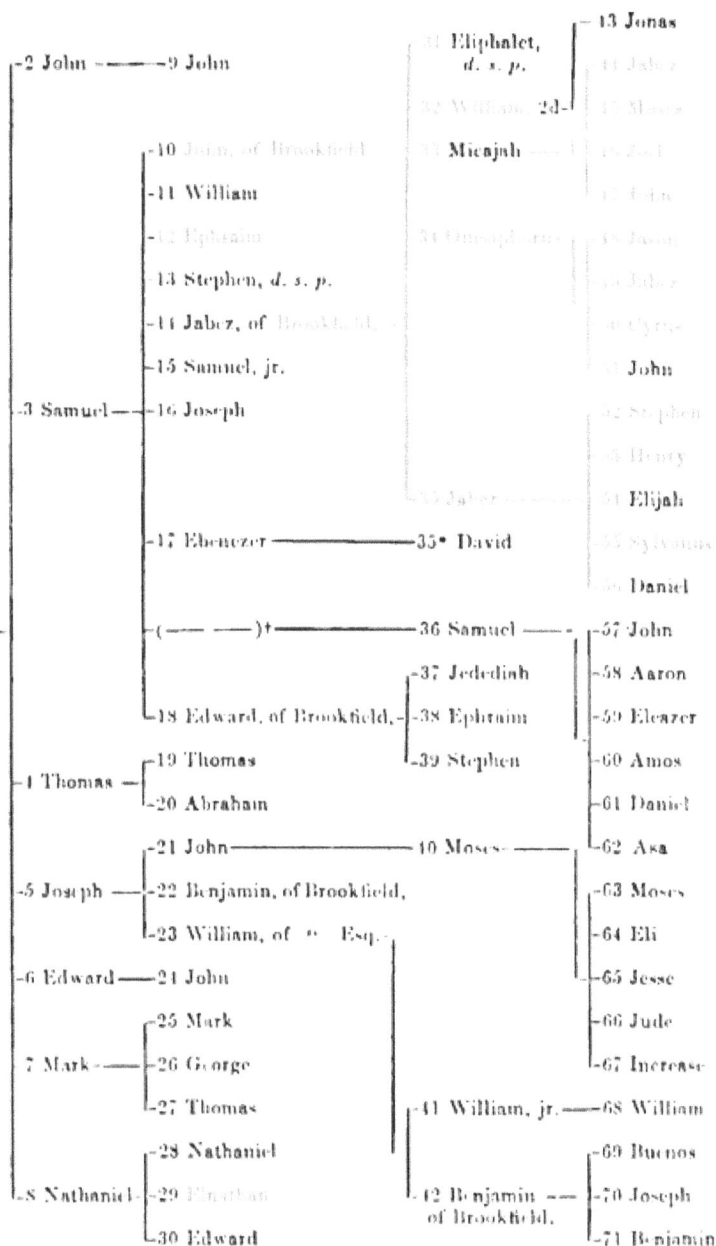

1 JOHN AYRES.

-2 John ——— -9 John

-3 Samuel
  -10 John, of Brookfield
  -11 William
  -12 Ephraim
  -13 Stephen, d. s. p.
  -14 Jabez, of Brookfield
  -15 Samuel, jr.
  -16 Joseph
  -17 Ebenezer ——— 35* David
  (—— ——)† ——— 36 Samuel
  -18 Edward, of Brookfield
    -37 Jedediah
    -38 Ephraim
    -39 Stephen

-4 Thomas
  -19 Thomas
  -20 Abraham

-5 Joseph
  -21 John ——— 40 Moses
  -22 Benjamin, of Brookfield
  -23 William, of "   Esq.

-6 Edward ——— 24 John

7 Mark
  -25 Mark
  -26 George
  -27 Thomas

-8 Nathaniel
  -28 Nathaniel
  -29 Jonathan
  -30 Edward

— 13 Jonas
31 Eliphalet, d. s. p.
32 William, 2d
33 Micajah
34 Onesiphorus
35 Jabez

-57 John
-58 Aaron
-59 Eleazer
-60 Amos
-61 Daniel
-62 Asa
-63 Moses
-64 Eli
-65 Jesse
-66 Jude
-67 Increase

-41 William, jr. ——— 68 William
-42 Benjamin ——
  of Brookfield.
-69 Buenos
-70 Joseph
-71 Benjamin

(right column, faded)
Jabez
Moses
John
Jason
Jabez
Cyrus
John
Stephen
Henry
Elijah
Sylvanus
Daniel

† SAMUEL 36 was a grandson of Samuel, but his father's name has not been found.

NOTE.

The following explanations may render the plan of the book more intelligible.

Each family is numbered in consecutive order, and this number will be found on some previous page, where the birth of the child was recorded. Thus on page 31 John Ayres is numbered 51, and by searching the margins back, on page 24 the number is placed against his name in the family of his father Onesiphorus. In the same way Onesiphorus 34 is found on page 17 in the record of *his* father Jabez 14.

The little figure following the name shows the generation in which the man belongs, counting our ancestor as the first. Thus John[5] Ayres is in the fifth generation, being son of Onesiphorus,[4] who was son of Jabez,[3] whose father Samuel[2] was son of Capt. John[1] Ayres.

The abbreviations are b. for born; d. for died; m. for married; unm. for unmarried; d. s. p. (*sine prole*) for died without children; pub. for published in marriage.

PREFACE

In the following pages an attempt has been made to record a portion of the descendants of Capt. John Ayres, one of the early colonists of New England. It is confessedly imperfect, and the main expectation of the compiler has been to prepare such an outline of the family history, especially in the earlier generations, as may enable others more directly interested in the subject to prepare a thorough record.

There have been several families in New England bearing names similar to Ayres, and as the spelling of this name has been varied, it has been difficult to keep the different families distinct on the records. Our family name has almost always preserved the final s, but it has often been spelt Eayres, Eyres, Eares, Ayers, &c.

Of families bearing a name similar but not identical, we may mention that of Eyre, descended from Dr. Simon Eyre, of Watertown, a family of high social position, now probably extinct in the male line.

We have next to notice the widely spread family descended from John Ayer, of Haverhill. This name has generally been spelt Ayers, and being found in Essex county at the same date that members of our family resided there, mistakes have been frequent in the genealogies hitherto published. I have however printed in the New England Historical and Genealogical

Register for October, 1863, a careful account of the grand-
children of John Ayer, and I trust future genealogists will be
spared these mistakes.

Of the name of Ayres, there were three early colonists between
whom no relationship is known or supposed to exist. These
were 1. Moses Ayres, of Dorchester, 1667, whose descendants
were of Boston ; 2. Samuel Ayres, of Ipswich, whose line
probably ceased after two generations : and 3. Capt. John Ayres,
of Ipswich, our progenitor.

It will not be necessary to trace the family of Moses Ayres,
and I will therefore briefly dispose of the line of

1. **Samuel**[1] **Ayres** of Ipswich. He had

    2   Samuel[2] b. 14 Sept. 1658.
    3   John[2] b. May, 1661.
    4   Joseph[2] b. 29 Oct. 1664.
         Mary[2] b. 22 June, 1667.
         Susan[2] b.   m. Thomas Wait, 21 Nov. 1677.

He probably m. a second wife, Mary Johnson, of Hampton,
14 Dec. 1681, and died 17 Feb. 1696–7.

2. **Samuel**[2] **Ayres**, jr. of Ipswich, m. probably widow Mary
Fuller, (published 23 June, 1721,) and had

         Samuel[3] b. 17 Feb. 1722-3 ;   d. 5 Dec. 1723.
         Lydia[3] b. 31 July, 1728 :   d. 10 Aug. 1728.
         Samuel[3] b. 8 Feb. 1729-30 ;   d. 12 March, 1729-30.
         Susanna b. 1 Oct. 1732 :   d. 12 Nov. 1732.

He died s. p. 21 Oct., 1743, aged 87. His will, proved 20
Oct., 1743, mentions his wife Mary, sister Mary, brother Joseph's
family, to whom he leaves property, giving his nephew Joseph a
double share. It is barely possible that he m. first Mary Johnson in 1681, but it is much more probable that she was the
second wife of Samuel[1] Ayres, Sr, as above noted.

3. **John¹ Ayres** of Ipswich, cordwainer, d. 23 Nov., 1690, and his brother Joseph was administrator. He was without doubt unmarried.

4. **Joseph¹ Ayres** of Ipswich, rider, m. Margery ———, and had

> Mary² b. 10 Aug. 1694.
> Sarah² b. 6 May, 1696.
> Elizabeth² b. 21 Sept. 1699.
> Deborah² b. 8 April, 1701.
> 5 Joseph² bapt. 4 Nov. 1705.

He died 4 March, 1730.

It appears, therefore, that of this family, Joseph Ayres, jr., who was living in 1743, being mentioned in his uncle's will, was the only grandson of Samuel Ayres, bearing the name. It has not seemed necessary to try to discover whether or not this Joseph has left any descendants.

* The name " Deborah " (daughter of Joseph, above), should be *Dorothy*. She m. prob. Charles Tuttle, jr., being pub. 30 Jan. 1730.

CAPT. JOHN[1] AYRES

was of Ipswich in 1648, and was then a tenant of John Norton's. I know nothing of his parentage, but it seems highly probable that he was accompanied hither by two of his brothers-in-law, William Lamson and William Fellows.*

He married Susanna, daughter of Mark Symonds, of Ipswich. This Mark Symonds, aged 50 years in 1654, died 28 Apr. 1659, leaving wife Joanna, daus. Susanna Ayres, Abigail, wife of Robert Pierce, Priscilla, wife of John Warner, and had had Mary, wife of, Edward Chapman, who died before her father. He may *possibly* have been a very distant relative of the noted Samuel Symonds, of Yeldham, co. Essex, and Ipswich, Mass.,—though there were several families of the name in New England not known to be connected.

John Ayres removed to Brookfield, Mass., when the settlement of that place was commenced, and in Nov. 1672, sold all his rights at Ipswich, including those "belonging to my father-in-law Mark Symonds,

---

* The ground for the conjecture is this. William Lamson died at Ipswich in 1659, leaving eight children. His wid. Sarah wished to marry one Thomas Hartshorn, but was opposed by *her brothers* William Fellows and John Ayres. Now as Ayres married a Symonds, and there is no record of any sisters of his wife who married Lamson and Fellows, it is fair to conclude that their wives were own sisters of John Ayres.

and used by me while I was a tenant upon Mr. John Norton's farm."

He was killed 3 Aug. 1675, with seven others, at the fight at Brookfield with the Indians. Though he had received large grants of land at Brookfield, some 2,000 acres, his family undoubtedly returned to Ipswich and its vicinity, the settlement having been broken up, and rendered unsafe.

His widow presented an inventory of his estate, now recorded at Salem, on which she wrote, "I have seven sons and one daughter." Although the births of these children are not all recorded, I have been able to recover all their names without doubt,* and I think to arrange them chronologically.

The children were

```
2   i   John 2
3   ii  Samuel 2
4   iii Thomas 2
5   iv  Joseph 2
6   v   Edward 2 b. 12 Feb. 1658.
7   vi  Mark 2 b. 14 Dec. 1661.        } all recorded at Ipswich.
8   vii Nathaniel 2 b. 6 July, 1664.
    viii Susanna 2 b.          ; m. ——— Day.
```

* The proofs are as follows:—The late SYLVESTER JUDD, of Northampton, sent me a copy of a petition, herein after quoted, made in 1717, by Thomas, Joseph, Mark, Nathaniel, and Edward Ayres for lands formerly granted their father John Ayres. In 1703 also, Samuel, John, and Thomas, were appointed executors of John, sr. Again in 1741 there was recorded at Worcester a deed dated 14 Jany 1716, from Thomas, Mark and Edward Ayres, all of Portsmouth, Nathaniel Ayres, of Boston, blacksmith, Samuel Ayres, of Ipswich, son of Samuel of the same, and Robert Day, of New Roxbury, "whose mother was Susanna Ayres,"—to Joseph Ayres, of Ipswich; it conveyed the land which was formerly possessed at Brookfield by their honored father John Ayres. The following is the petition above mentioned.

October 28th, 1717.

A Petition of Thomas Ayres, Joseph Ayres, Mark Ayres, Natt'll Ayres, & Edward Ayres, Sons & Heirs of John Ayres heretofore of Qualoag alias Brookfield, Dec'd Intestate, Shewing that in or about the Year 1660, the Petitioners Father with others bought & purchased of the Indian

Susanna **Ayres**, widow of John, died at Ipswich, 8 Feb. 1682–3. In October previous, Mrs. Rebecca Symonds had given her a portion of a fund sent to be distributed among the sufferers from fires and the Indians.

SECOND GENERATION.

2. John² Ayres was of Ipswich, and had a wife, Mary, and children recorded there, viz.

9 i John³ b. Sept. 1677;   the entry of the name is torn.
  ii Abigail³ b. 14 May, 1680;
  iii Ruth³ b. 22 Nov. 1685 ;   d. 24 Dec. 1685, called daughter
                               of John and Mary Ayres.

Natives a Tract of Land of about Eight Miles square then known & called by the Name of Quoboag, After which, Viz. in the Year 1673, the General Court erected the said Land into a Township by the Name of Brookfield, That in the Year 1675, A War broke out with the Indians, who kill'd Petitioners Father & several other Inhabitants, And the Rest being drawn off by Order of the Government, the whole Town was left desolate, and all the Houses burnt Down by the Enemy, After which, about 1690, the said Town of Brookfield was in a likely Way to be settled. And in the Year 1703 the Petitioners having obtained Administration on their Fathers Estate lying in Brookfield afore said, petitioned the Gen'll Court that a Committee might be appointed to make Enquiry & Cause a Record to be made of the Lots Rights & Proprieties of Land within the said Plantation belonging to the ancient Settlers thereof, that so the Petitioners might have & enjoy what belong'd to them in Right of their Father, W'ch Prayer of the Petitioners was accordingly granted, & Sam'll Patridge Esq'r & others appointed a Comm'tee were ordered to make Enquiry & Cause a Record to be made of the said Lots, Rights, and Proprieties, But the said Committee neglecting that Service, the Petitioners renewed their Petition to the Gen'll Court, who appointed a Hearing thereon; However the Petitioners withdrew their Petition at the Request of the said Committee, & upon their Promise that they would forthwith proceed to settle the Petitioners in their Rights, Which accordingly they did to the Satisfaction of the Petitioners, who were at the Expence of One Hundred & fifty Pounds at least in Obtaining the said Settlement, But after all the Committee did in March last declare all their Proceedings in the Premisses to be null & void under no other Pretence, but that the said Lands were not improved by the Petitioners, And the very Lots that the Petitioners Father died possess'd of, & particularly his Home Lot which he defended against the Indians to

I do not find that any children of his claimed lands
at Brookfield, and I am inclined to believe that he
moved to Boston, where a John Ayres died 12 Aug.
1711, aged 62, who by his will, dated two days before,
left all his property to his wife Mary.* It will be
remembered that John's brother Nathaniel was of
Boston.

3. Samuel ² Ayres of Newbury and Rowley,
married at Ipswich 16 April, 1677, Abigail, daughter

the Loss of his Life are granted by the said Committee to other Persons
very unjustly & contrary to the Order of the Gen'll Assembly, By all w'ch
the Petitioners are kept out of the Possession of their Fathers Estate.

Upon the Whole the Petitioners pray the Hon'ble Court will confirm to
them the Lands which the said Committee have laid out to them Containing
by Estimation no more than Fifteen or Sixteen Hundred Acres, Altho' they
have heard their Father & many others say That he had Two Thousand
Acres of Land in Brookfield. With which Land so laid out by the said
Committee they shall rest satisfied & contented, Unless the Court shall
please to make them some further Consideration:

Read in the House of Representatives Oct 26, 1717, And Ordered, that
the Committee of Brookfield be served with a Copy of this & the Petitioners
former Petition, And that they appear before this Court on the second
Thursday of the next May Session, to shew Reason why they declared the
Petition'rs land to be forfeited.

Sent up for Concurrence: Read & Concur'd.

Consented to, Sam'll Shute.

[I am indebted for this copy from Records of Gov. and Council in Office of
Sec. of Commonwealth, Vol. X. to my friend A. C. GOODELL, jr., of Salem.]

* It must be said, however, that a John and Bridget Ayres, of Boston,
had Bridget, b. 20 June, 1679, and Elizabeth b. 28 Sept. 1683. We find
also on the Boston records:

1677–8   2 Jany, Abigail Ayres aged 27, died.
1677–8   3 Mch. sister Ayres joined the Second Church.
1699   28 Dec. Ann Ayres m. John Lawson.
1714–5   8 Mch. Elizabeth A. m. Capt Thomas Allen of Truro.
1720   4 July, Sarah A. m. Thomas Allen.

From these proofs that other families of Ayres lived in Boston, I am
led to leave this identification of John who died in 1711 still unsettled.

He died prior to Oct. 1717, and his widow was alive in 1722; we have not found the exact dates of the death of either.

The intimacy between Samuel Ayres and his brother-in-law Fellows was so great that it may confirm our supposition that they were cousins. May 23, 1701, Samuel Fellows, Sr., late of Ipswich, now of Newbury, gave land left by his father William Fellows, in his will of 29 Nov. 1686, "in consequence of the many kindnesses shown me by my loving brother-in-law Samuel Ayres, Sr., of Newbury, who married my sister," and "especially in consideration of an agreement he hath made this day with his sons Samuel Ayres, Jr., and John Ayres, to maintain me."

* The records say that Jabez was son of Samuel and Sarah Ayres. Yet this is undoubtedly a clerical error, since Samuel's widow was named Abigail, and she calls herself mother of Stephen, elder brother of Jabez. Other proofs might be added, but especially it seems unnecessary to suppose that Samuel had three wives, two named Abigail, when there is no trace of any indication of any such fact. The first time Abigail Ayres appears is in a deed dated 5 Oct. 1717, (Essex Deeds, vol. 38, p. ...) by which Abigail widow of Samuel, together with John Ayres and Edward Ayres of the second name, the mother and brothers of Stephen Ayres, late of ..., give up their claims to his widow Martha. A similar power is given by Samuel, Joseph, John, Ebenezer, Jabez and Edward Ayres, brothers of the deceased. [Essex Deeds, vol. 37, p. 115.]

In 1704-5, Samuel Ayres, Jr., and John Ayres, both of Rowley, bought land on which to support their parents, Samuel and Abigail Ayres.

4. **Thomas**[2] **Ayres** of Newbury and Ipswich. married Hannah Errington, 21 Mch 1677-8, and had

19   i   Thomas[3] b. 25 Jan. 1678-9.   mentioned in grants of 1714.
      ii   Hannah[3] b. 2 Aug. 1680.
     iii   Rebecca[3] b. 27 May, 1682.
     iv   a dau[3] b. June, 1686,   (at Ipswich) possibly this was
         Susanna   whom. 1st, William Scales,
                             and 2d, Cornelius Soule,
                             of North Yarmouth.
20   v   Abraham[3] b. 18 June, 1688; mentioned in grants, 1714.
      vi   Sarah[3] b. 29 Aug. 1690.
     vii   Mehitable[3] b. 5 April, 1697.

He was of Portsmouth in 1717. (see Middlesex Deeds. xx. 549.) Besides his two sons, grants were made at Brookfield, 1717, to sons-in-law William Scales and Joseph Moses. In 1729, (Worcester Records. iii. 277.) Cornelius Soule, of North Yarmouth, and wife Susanna, widow of Wm. Scales, sell land at Brookfield.

5. **Joseph**[2] **Ayres** of Ipswich married 9 June, 1681. Sarah Caldwell, and had

      i   Sarah[3] b. 5 Aug. 1685.
     ii   Elizabeth[3] b. 28 Jan. 1687-8 ;   m. Aaron Kimball, 5 Feb.
21   iii   John[3] b. 26 Feb. 1692-3.   [1716-17.
22   iv   Benjamin[3] b. 13 Sept. 1696.
23   v   William[3] b. 16 Dec. 1700.

I think he married a second wife. widow Hannah Dutch. pub. 21 Apr. 1710. He removed to Brookfield. having as before recorded. purchased the claims of his brothers. He d. 3 Nov. 1740; his wife d. July. 1740.

6. Edward[2] Ayres of Kittery, Me., had

24	i	John[3]	; had grant at Brookfield, 1717.
	ii	Elizabeth[3]	; prob. m. Caleb Griffith, 30 Oct. 1701.
	iii	a dau.[3]	; m. Joseph Moulton, as appears by grants. In 1699 he had a grant of 20 acres in Kittery.

7. Mark[2] Ayres of Kittery, Me.,* had as it appears by the Brookfield grants, 1717, three sons.

25	i	Mark.[3]
26	ii	George.[3]
27	iii	Thomas.[3]

8. Nathaniel Ayres of Boston, m. Amy ——— and had

28	i	Nathaniel.	
	ii	Amy[3]	; m. Samuel Swasey, 16 Jan. 1710-11.
29	iii	Elnathan.[3]	
30	iv	Edward.[3]	
	v	a dau[3]	; m. Jethro Furbur, of Portsmouth, N. H., 1732, as per grants.

He died 4 Dec. 1737, aged 67 years, 6 months.

* As to the Kittery branch, Nathaniel and Mark were of N. H. in 1690, and Nathaniel was a sergeant, 1695, and in 1699 a justice of the peace. Hannah A., m. Edward Toogood at Portsmouth, 16 Oct., 1711, and Rebecca A., m. Joseph Moses, 17 Aug., 1712. Edward Ayres, of Newington, m. Mary Row, 1 Nov., 1712, Samuel A., m. Phebe Neal, 7 April, 1715, Stephen A., m. Sarah Hoyden, 2 Sept., 1773; these last were of Portsmouth. John Ayres, of N. H., was in 1745 a soldier at Louisburg. James A., of Greenland, m. Mary Neal, 6 Sept., 1760.

THIRD GENERATION.

[Issue of John.²]

9. John³ Ayres [of Boston?]

If John² Ayres, the eldest son of Capt. John Ayres, had any son, a fact which is still in doubt, I should be inclined to identify him with John Ayres, of Boston, who m. Elizabeth Halsie, there, 20 Dec. 1706, and who probably had

> Mary⁴ bapt. 12 Oct 1707, at the Second Church, in right of the mother Elizabeth.

This John doubtless joined the same church, 5 Nov. 1710. If he were the son of John and Mary, I should presume that he died before his father, 13 Aug. 1711, as before cited.

John Ayres, jr., had a grant at Brookfield in 1720-1. Still, I am inclined to think this was John, (21) son of Joseph, whose older cousin John, (10) son of Samuel, was living at the same time in the same town.

My conviction is strong that the line of John Ayres, the oldest son of Capt. John, became extinct before 1711.

[Issue of Samuel.²]

10. John³ Ayres of Rowley 1705, and Brookfield, had wife Hannah ——, and by her had

> Hannah⁴ b. 9 July, 1715;   d. Oct. 31, 1725.

He died 18 Dec. 1739. His widow's will of 13 May, 1747, mentions Abigail, dau. of Edward Ayres, "my late husband John Ayres' neice," and John Ayres, a minor aged 5 years, son of Samuel Ayres, "my late husband's nephew." This is a proof that this John was brother of Jabez, Edward, &c., and a son of Samuel[2] Ayres. Additional proof that he was not John, son of Joseph,[2] is that the widow appoints her *friend* William[3] Ayres (son of Joseph[2]) executor. She would not thus have spoken of a brother-in-law probably.

11. William[3] Ayres of Ipswich.

12. Ephraim[3] Ayres of Ipswich.

13. Stephen[3] Ayres of Newbury and Gloucester, m. Martha Caldwell, pub. at Ipswich, 28 Feb. 1712.

He died undoubtedly *s. p.*, about 12 April, 1720, when administration was granted. He could have had no children since his brothers and mother were the heirs, and as we have seen released their right to his widow.

14. Jabez[3] Ayres of Newbury, m. Dec. 8, 1718, Rebecca, dau. of Henry Kimball, and had

  i Stephen[4] b. 3 Aug. 1719 ; d. young.
31   ii Eliphalet[4] b. 4 March, 1722-3.
32   iii William[4] b. 28 Feb. 1723-4.
33   iv Micajah[4] b. 24 Sept. 1729.
34   v Onesiphorus[4] b. 7 April, 1733.
  vi Stephen[4] b. 1 Feb. 1734-5 ; d. young.
35   vii Jabez[4] b. 26 April, 1737.

He removed to Brookfield, having sold out June 5, 1721, the land he acquired with his wife. (See Essex Deeds, xi, 212.) Jabez Ayres and wife Rebecca, dau. of said Henry Kimball, sell to Nathaniel Peasley, land bought by " our honoured father, Henry Kimball, late of Haverhill, deceased."

15. Samuel[5] **Ayres** of Ipswich, termed jr., married Eleanor Randall, 7 June, 1705. Whether they had children elsewhere does not appear, but at Ipswich they had

> i Martha[4] bapt. 2 March, 1717-8.
> ii John[4] bapt. 22 Nov. 1719 ;   died 20 Feb. 1720-1.
> iii John[4] bapt. 17 Sept. 1721.
> iv Elizabeth[4] bapt. 6 Oct. 1723 ;   d. 9 Oct. 1723.
> v Mary[4] bapt. 4 April, 1725.

Eleanor, wife of Samuel Ayres, jr., died at Ipswich, 21 Oct. 1734, and he doubtless m. Hannah Gold, published 31 Dec. 1737. He was of Rowley 1705.

16. Joseph **Ayres** of Ipswich.

17. Ebenezer[5] **Ayres** of Newbury, m. Dorcas Getchell, of Salisbury, 5 Oct. 1710, and had

> 35   David[4] b. 11 Aug. 1711.

By Worcester Deeds, (i. 227,) he sold in 1731 land that he bought of his brother, John Ayres, and land laid out to himself.

18. Edward[1] **Ayres** of Brookfield, m. Jemima Davis there, 19 Nov. 1718, and had

    i William[4] b. 16 Dec. 1719;   d. 20 Oct. 1721.
    ii John[4] b. 10 Jan. 1721-2.
    iii Abigail[4] b. 13 Feb. 1723-4.
    iv Hannah[4] b. 2 May, 1726;   d. 25 Oct. 1738.
    v Samuel[4] b. 25 Feb. 1727-8; d. 24 Oct. 1739.
37 vi Jedediah[4] b. 7 Sept. 1729.
38 vii Ephraim[4] b. 13 June, 1733.*
    viii Edward[4] b. 31 Jan. 1734-5.
39 ix Stephen[4] b.

[Issue of Thomas.[2]]

19. Thomas[3] **Ayres** of Ipswich.

20. Abraham[3] **Ayres** of Ipswich.

[Issue of Joseph.[2]]

21. John[3] **Ayres** of Brookfield, and wife Mercy, had there the following:—

    i Mary[4] b. 24 Aug. 1719;   d. 15 Sept. 1721.
    ii Benjamin[4] b. 25 Aug. 1723; d. 30 May, 1736.
40 iii Moses[4] b. 3 Dec. 1725.

March 4, 1724-5, administration on the estate of John of Brookfield was granted to Ebenezer Ayres of Brookfield. His son Moses is mentioned on the Proprietor's Record in 1748.

22. Benjamin[3] **Ayres** of Brookfield had a grant in 1714. He d. 23 May, 1717; prob. unm.

---

* Of Ware river parish, 1757, being about to serve under Lord Loudon, made his will, mentions bros. Jedediah and Stephen.

23. **William** [3] **Ayres** of Brookfield, called Capt. and Esquire, a prominent man among the early settlers of the reorganized town. He m. 1st, 8 Jan., 1724–5, Hannah Hamelton, and had

i Hannah [4] b. 11 Oct. 1725 ;	m. —— Gould.
ii Sarah [4] b. 17 Sept. 1727 ;	m. —— Sprague.
iii Joseph [4] b. 19 Nov. 1729 ;	d 21 April, 1768, (tombstone.) prob. unm.
iv Mary [4] b. 22 Dec. 1731 ;	m. Joseph Locke of Shutesbury. pub. May, 1754.
41 v William [4] b. 1 May, 1734.	
vi Elizabeth [4] b. 27 April, 1736.	
vii Olive [4] b. 14 May, 1737 ;	m. Ephraim Wheeler, 9 Dec. 1761.
42 viii Benjamin [4] b. 15 Oct. 1741 ;	d. before his father.
ix Lydia [4] b. 21 Nov. 1743 ;	m. Jonathan Wyman.
x Increase [4] b. 17 June, 1748;	d. 21 May, 1767, (tombstone.)

His wife d. 8 Dec. 1748, aged 43, and he m. 2d, Persis Rice, 3 Jan. 1753, who d. prob. *s. p.* 9 Jan. 1756, aged 33. He m. lastly, Mrs. Mary Wolcott, 23 Dec. 1772, who survived him. He died 19 Aug. 1789, aged 88. (These deaths are from the tombstones at Brookfield.) His will, dated 26 May, 1787, mentions wife Mary, William, son of his son William, deceased, and Miriam, widow of William, now wife of Joseph Barns. Daus. Lydia Wyman, Hannah Gould, Mary Locke, Sarah Sprague, Olive Wheeler, and grand children by them. *

[Nos. 24—27. Issue of Edward [2] and Mark [2] of Kittery untraced.]

* His will also mentions his grand-children, the children of son Benjamin, deceased, specifying especially Joseph and Benjamin, who were probably minors.

[Issue of Nathaniel Ayres, 18.]

28. Nathaniel Ayres of Boston, m. 5 Nov. 1724, Elizabeth Kitts, and had

     i John b. 12 March, 1725-6.
     ii Joseph b. 24 Jan. 1726-7.
     iii Margaret b. 31 Aug. 1729.
     iv Nathaniel b. 31 Aug. 1734.

29. Elnathan Ayres of Boston, m. 1 July, 1720, Mary Jones, and had

     i Nathaniel b. 5 Jan. 1722-3
     ii Ammi (Amy?) b. 29 Feb. 1727-8.

30. Edward Ayres of Boston, m. 25 April, 1716, Rebecca Marshall, and had

     i Mary b. 16 Feb. 1716-7.
     ii Edward b. 14 Jan. 1720-1; d.

He m. 2d, 5 Nov. 1724, Hannah Eveleth, and had

     i Edward b. 19 Aug. 1725.
     ii Hannah b. 15 May, 1727
     iii Sarah b. 2 Oct. 1729.
     iv John b. 12 April, 1733.
     v Joseph b. 11 April, 1743.

His widow proved his will, 8 Nov. 1743.

[These Boston families have probably living representatives.]

BROOKFIELD BRANCH.

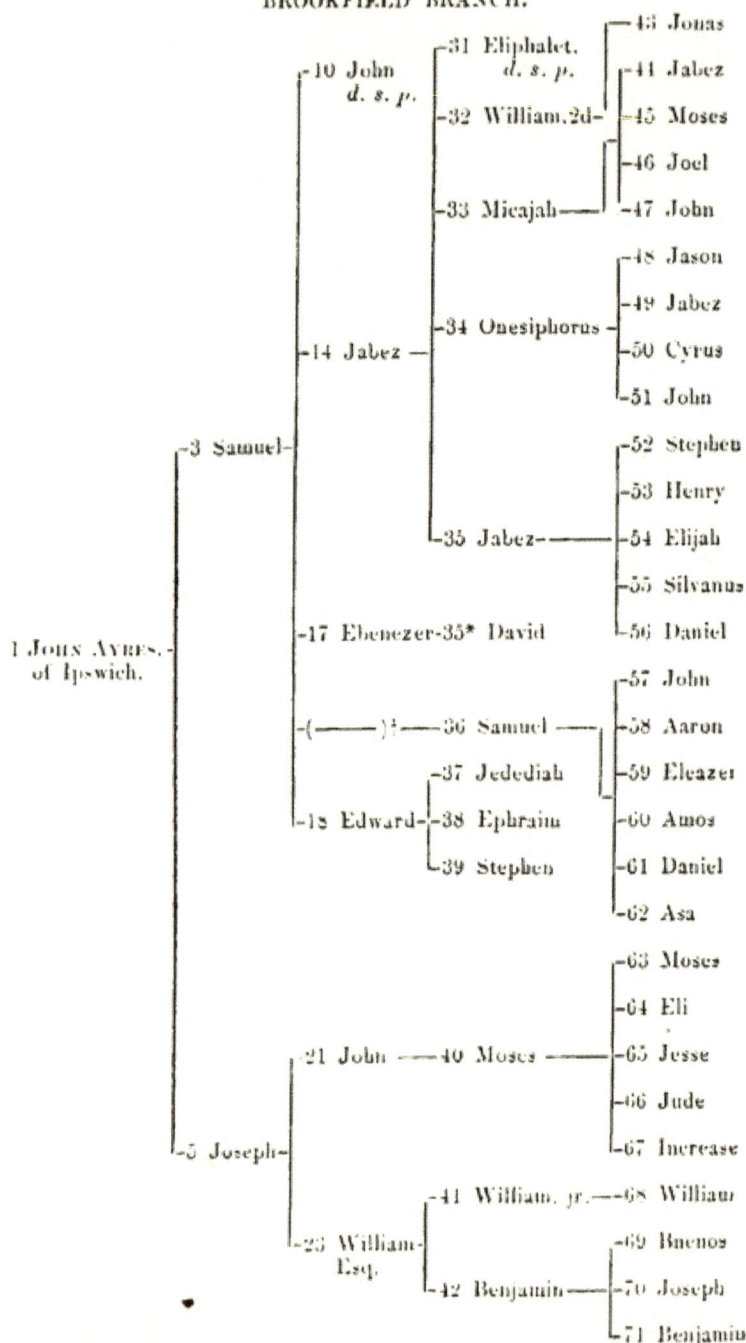

```
                                          ┌─43 Jonas
                              ┌─31 Eliphalet.
                  ┌─10 John   │    d. s. p.  ┌─44 Jabez
                  │  d. s. p. ├─32 William,2d─┤
                  │           │              └─45 Moses
                  │           │              ┌─46 Joel
                  │           └─33 Micajah───┤
                  │                          └─47 John
                  │                          ┌─48 Jason
                  │                          │
                  │              ┌─34 Onesiphorus─┤─49 Jabez
                  ├─14 Jabez ────┤              ├─50 Cyrus
                  │              │              └─51 John
                  │              │              ┌─52 Stephen
      ┌─3 Samuel──┤              │              │
      │           │              │              ├─53 Henry
      │           │              └─35 Jabez─────┤─54 Elijah
      │           │                             ├─55 Silvanus
      │           │                             └─56 Daniel
      │           ├─17 Ebenezer-35* David       ┌─57 John
      │           │                             │
1 JOHN AYRES,─────┤           ┌─36 Samuel ──────┤─58 Aaron
   of Ipswich.    │  ─(──── )‡─┤                 ├─59 Eleazer
      │           │           ├─37 Jedediah     │
      │           └─18 Edward─┤─38 Ephraim      ├─60 Amos
      │                        └─39 Stephen     ├─61 Daniel
      │                                         └─62 Asa
      │                                         ┌─63 Moses
      │                                         │
      │                                         ├─64 Eli
      │              ┌─21 John ──40 Moses ──────┤─65 Jesse
      │              │                          ├─66 Jude
      └─5 Joseph─────┤                          └─67 Increase
                     │           ┌─41 William. jr.──68 William
                     │           │                 ┌─69 Buenos
                     └─23 William─┤                │
                        Esq.      └─42 Benjamin────┤─70 Joseph
                                                   └─71 Benjamin
```

* SAMUEL 36 was a grandson of Samuel, but his father's name has not been found.

FOURTH GENERATION.

We propose now to trace only those descendants of Capt. John Ayres who were settled in Worcester county near Brookfield.

These were the grandsons of Samuel and Joseph, and were sons of Jabez, (14) and Edward, (18) and of their cousins John, (21) and William, (23). A glance at the Chart will explain this, and I may add, that in my investigations I have found a recognition of there being two families or branches at Brookfield. Thus William Ayres (23) the " Squire" was known to be *not* the brother of Jabez, (14) and the descendants of each recognized the fact that their cousins of the name in the other branch were farther removed. We will therefore consider each of the families separately.

[Children of Jabez³ Ayres, (14).]

31. Eliphalet⁴ Ayres of New Braintree, m. Catharine Allen, 13 Sept. 1758, and had

    i John⁵ b. 30 June, 1759 ; killed in the Revolutionary War.

Eliphalet then adopted his nephew Moses⁵ Ayres, son of Micajah. His wife d. May, 1792, and he d. 3 Oct. 1796.

32. William⁴ Ayres of Brookfield, (known as William Ayres, 2nd, and Lieut.) m. Rachel Barns, 3 July, 1753, and had

    i Rebecca⁵ b. 18 March, 1754 ; m. Remalay.
    ii Beulah⁵ b. 24 Aug. 1756 ; d. 24 March, 1777.
    iii Hannah⁵ b. 14 Aug. 1758 ; m. Nath'l Belknap, (pub. 10 Sept. 1776).
    iv Eunice⁵ b. 24 Jan. 1761 ; m. Mason.
    v Susan⁵ b. 22 Feb. 1763 ; d. unm. 20 Sept. 1852.
    vi John⁵ b. 29 March, 1765 ; d. 16 April, 1765

    vii Rufus⁵ b. 10 March, 1766 ;   d. 2 May, 1766.
    viii Hazelelponi⁵ b. 13 April, 1767 : d. unm. 23 Feb. 1834.
43 ix Jonas⁵ b. 10 Sept. 1769.
    x Joel⁵ b. 2 May, 1772 ;   d. young.
    xi Kate⁵ b. 8 Aug. 1773 ;   d 9 Sept. 1773.
    xii David⁵ b. 29 Oct. 1774 ;   d. 19 Nov. 1774.
    xiii Lydia⁵ b. 22 July. 1776.
    xiv John⁵ b. 28 Feb. 1778 ;   d. 8 March, 1778.

He died 31 Dec. 1814; his widow d. 24 May, 1817.

33. Micajah⁴ Ayres of New Braintree, m. 14 March, 1764, Sarah Barnes, and had

44 i Jabez⁵ b. 13 Feb. 1765.
45 ii Moses⁵ b. 23 Aug. 1766.
    iii Sarah⁵ b. 13 Dec. 1768.
    iv Rebecca⁵ b. 26 Dec. 1769 ;   m.   Luce.
46 v Joel.⁵
47 vi John.⁵

He died at New Braintree, 27 Jan. 1804, aged 74 years, and his wife d. 16 April, 1799.

34. Onesiphorus⁴ Ayres m. 6 Dec. 1759, Anna Goodale, and had

48 i Jason⁵ b. 16 March. 1761.
    ii Judith⁵ b. 12 Jan. 1763 ;   m. Dr. Jason Tyler, of Chesterfield, N. H.
    iii Anna⁵ b. 10 Oct. 1764 ;   m. John Rainger, jr., (pub. 16 Oct. 1785.)
49 iv Jabez⁵ b. 5 Dec. 1766.
    v Louisa⁵ b. 23 Nov. 1768 ;   m. Joseph Snow, (pub. 6 Oct. 1788.)
    vi Matilda⁵ b. 27 July, 1771 ;   m. Josiah Convers, of Bakerfield, Vt.
50 vii Cyrus⁵ b. 28 Nov. 1773.
    viii Sarah⁵ b. 10 June, 1776 ;   m. Joshua Howe, (pub. 25 Dec. 1796.)
51 ix John⁵ b. 10 April. 1779.
    x Amy⁵ b. 12 May, 1781 ;   m. Merrick Rice.

He d. 2 June, 1809.   His widow d. 13 June, 1811.

35. Jabez⁴ Ayres of New Braintree, m. Persis Stewart, and had

	i	Ebenezer⁵ b.	1767 ;	d. unm. in 1837, at Manheim.
52	ii	Stephen⁵ b.	1770.	
	iii	Alexander⁵ b.	1772 ;	d. unm. at Salisbury.
53	iv	Henry⁵ b.	1774	
54	v	Elijah⁵ b.	1778.	
55	vi	Silvanus⁵ b. April.	1780.	
	vii	Mary⁵ b.	1782 ;	m. { 1st, Alvin Case. { 2d, Comfort Case.
56	viii	Daniel⁵ b. 17 May,	1787.	

He was a soldier in the French and Indian War and in the Revolution. He removed from New Braintree in 1792, to Salisbury, Herkimer co., New York, thence to Manheim in the same county, and died there 24 Feb. 1824. His widow d. in 1833, aged 68.

35*. David⁴ Ayres, [probably son of Ebenezer,³ (17).] m. at New Braintree, 20 April, 1757, Elizabeth [penny,] and 17 March 1768, Mary Perkins. Nothing more appears concerning him.

36. Samuel⁴ Ayres of Brookfield and Granby, weaver, m. Martha Bell, 21 Jan. 1742, and had

57	i	John⁵ b. 29 Dec. 1742 ;	m. Ruth Smith.
58	ii	Aaron⁵ b. 12 Nov. 1744 ;	m. { Lois Moody. { Mary Hitchcock.
59	iii	Eleazer⁵ b. 20 Dec. 1746;	m. Sybil Clark.
60	iv	Amos⁵ b. 16 April. 1749 ;	m. Esther Dickinson.
61	v	Daniel⁵ b. 15 July, 1751 ;	m.
	vi	Sarah⁵ b. 10 May, 1754 ;	d. 26 April, 1776.
	vii	Lydia⁵ b. 22 Sept 1756 ;	m. Chilion Palmer.
	viii	Susannah⁵ b. 28 Jan. 1759.	d. 7 Jan. 1771.
62	ix	Asa⁵ b. 5 June, 1761 ;	m. Mary Wait.
	x	Martha⁵ b. 22 Sept. 1763.	m. Asher Alvord.

He was drowned 15 Nov. 1768, aged 52; his wife d. 25 Oct. 1765, aged 41.

By the will of the widow of John Ayres, (10) of Brookfield, it is clear that this Samuel was his nephew, and we therefore place him here. He is also termed nephew by John in 1739, Worcester Deeds, ii, 3. We have not found out which one of John's brothers was the father of this Samuel.

(Numbers 37, 38 and 39, are untraced.)

[Grandsons of Joseph² Ayres, (5).]

40. Capt. Moses⁴ Ayres of Brookfield, m. Sarah Converse, and had

	i	John⁵ b. 21 July, 1749 ;	d. 10 Nov. 1757.
63	ii	Moses⁵ b. 30 Jan. 1751.	
	iii	Sarah⁵ b. 30 March, 1753.	
	iv	Jesse⁵ b. 20 May, 1755 ;	d. 27 Oct. 1757.
	v	John⁵ b. 21 Nov. 1758 ;	d. 30 May, 1778.
64	vi	Eli⁵ b. 27 Feb. 1761.	
65	vii	Jesse⁵ b. 8 Oct. 1763.	
66	viii	Jude⁵ b. 12 March, 1766.	
67	ix	Increase⁵ b. 16 Nov. 1768.	
	x	Abigail	; m. Peter Washburn.

He d. 6 Dec. 1796; his widow d. 22 Nov. 1825.

41. William⁴ Ayres, jr. of Brookfield, (son of Squire William,) m. Miriam ———, and had

	i	Elizabeth⁵ b. 28 Oct. 1762.	d. unm. 26 July, 1842.
68	ii	William⁵ b. 23 July, 1765.	

He d. 14 June, 1767. His widow m. Joseph Barnes.

42. Benjamin¹ Ayres of Brookfield, (son of Squire William,) died before his father; in the will of the latter, dated in 1787, he mentions his grandchildren Joseph and Benjamin, sons of his son Benjamin deceased, and also other children unnamed. Benjamin m. 12 Nov. 1762, Beulah Crosby, and had

69   i Buenos⁵ b. May, 1763.
     ii Thomas⁵ b. 24 May, 1765.
     iii Persis⁵ b. 6 April, 1767
70   iv Joseph⁵ b. 24 June, 1769.
     v Relief⁵ b. 15 Jan. 1772.
     vi Mary⁵ b. 29 Sept. 1779.
71   vii Benjamin⁵   ; mentioned in will.

He d. 1 June, 1785.

NOTE.—A Joseph Ayres of New Braintree, m. Mary Gibson, 1774, and had Adin, b. 18 July, 1775. I know nothing more of them.

FIFTH GENERATION.

43. Jonas **Ayres** of Brookfield. m. 6 March, 1800, Hannah Winslow, and had

 i Joshua-Winslow b. 27 Dec.
  1800 ;   d. unm. 20 Feb. 1822.
 ii Hannah b. 21 March, 1802 ; m. Ira Greenwood, 13 Oct.
            1835.
 iii Isabelle b. 1 Nov. 1803 : d. unm. 6 May, 1868.
 iv Abigail b. 30 Sept. 1805 : d. unm. 17 Nov. 1836.
 v Rachel b. 26 Oct. 1807 ; m. Joel Sampson, 26 Feb.
            1833.
72 vi William-Henry b. 5 March, 1810.
 vii Sarah b. 17 March, 1812 ; m. Geo. Hollister, 8 July,
            1851.
 viii Harriet-Newell b. 10 July, 1816.

He d. 17 Nov. 1840; his wife d. 3 Oct. 1836.

44. Jabez **Ayres** of New Braintree. m. Eunice Goodnow, in 1791, (pub. 4 April,) and had

73 i Perley b. 30 April, 1792.
74 ii Isaac b. 29 July, 1793.
 iii Miranda }
 iv Maria } b. 8 May, 1795.
75 v Elias b. 9 Nov. 1798.
 vi Nahum b. 19 March, 1802 ; m. 1st, Sarah King : m. 2d.
           Eliz. Anderson, and d.
           s. p. 24 Aug. 1860.
 vii Hiram b. 13 May, 1804 ; d. unm. Nov. 1827.

He d. at New Braintree, 26 March, 1847, aged 82.

45. Moses **Ayres** of New Braintree. m. 1st. Rhoda Mathews, 3 Oct. 1789, and had

 i Sarah b.

He m. 2d, Sarah Edmunds, 3 Oct. 1795, and had

 ii Samuel⁶ b.   d. young.
76 iii John⁶ b.
 iv Mary Ann⁶ b. 6 Dec. 1798
 v Priscilla Elora⁶ b. 5 Nov. 1802; d. unm. 28 July, 1804, aged 61.
 vi Moses⁶ b. 12 May, 1805 d. unm. 7 Sept. 1865
 vii Ormusinda⁶ b. 9 May, 1808; m. Wm. Johnson, 2d wife, Feb. 1830
 viii Julia Ann⁶ b. 2 April, 1810; m. Wm. Johnson, 1st wife.

He d. 19 Feb. 1844, aged 77, and his widow d. 3 Oct. 1850, aged 87; both at New Braintree.

46. Joel⁵ Ayres of Hardwick, Mass., Royalston, Weybridge and Vergennes, Vt., m. 16 Oct. 1796, Bathsheba Jordan, and had

77 i Anson⁶ b. 1797.
78 ii Tilly⁶ b. 14 Feb. 1799.
79 iii Hiram⁶ b. 28 Dec. 1801.
80 iv Eli⁶ b. 24 Nov. 1802.
81 v Joseph⁶ b. 17 Oct. 1804.
82 vi Francis⁶ b. 5 March, 1807.
83 vii Jefferson⁶ b. 13 Feb. 1809
84 viii Dudley J.⁶ b. 11 March, 1811.
 ix Alma⁶ b. 1813; m. Rev. Hiram Blanchard

His wife d. 28 Aug. 1819, and he m. 2d, widow Scott, Dec. 1819, and had

 x Eveline⁶ b. 1821; m. H. H. Stephens

He m. thirdly, widow Munger, Jan. 1824, and had
 xi Minerva⁶ b. 1 June, 1828; m. M. F. Collins, 2 Jan. 1849.

He d. 19 June, 1846; his widow d. Nov., 1865.

47. John⁵ Ayres. m. Alpha Kelly, and had two sons, but I have not the record of them.

He went to Maine to live, but afterwards moved to Virgil, Courtland co. New York, and probably died there.

48. Dr. Jason⁵ Ayres of Brookfield, Phillipston and Truro, Mass., m. Betsey Holman, 17 April, 1791, and had

	i	Cullen⁶ b. 11 Aug. 1793 ;	d. unm. 10 June. 1819.
	ii	Olive⁶ b. 10 July, 1794 ;	m. Samuel Rider.
	iii	Horace⁶ b. 18 April, 1796 ;	d. unm. 19 April, 1817.
	iv	Adeline⁶ b. 6 Aug. 1799 ;	d. 7 Sept. 1803.
	v	Betsey⁶ b. 10 April, 1802 ;	d. 8 Aug. 1803.
	vi	John⁶ b. 21 Dec. 1804 ;	d. 4 April, 1806.
85	vii	Marshall⁶ b. 28 June, 1807.	
86	viii	Dana⁶ b. 7 Dec. 1809.	
	ix	Sally⁶ b. 8 June, 1814 ;	m. Josiah Lombard.

He lived also in Truro, Mass., but d. in Griggsville, Ill., 29 July, 1838; his wife d. in Truro, 12 Dec. 1831.

49. Jabez⁵ Ayres of Brookfield, m. Hannah Gilbert, 3 Dec. 1795, and had

	i	Anu⁶ b. 27 Feb. 1797 ;	m. Levi Bush.
87	ii	Baxter⁶ b. 5 June, 1799.	
	iii	Betsey⁶ b. 7 Oct. 1801 ;	m. Luther Brigham.
	iv	Stillman⁶ b. 8 Aug. 1803 ;	d. unm. 6 July, 1819.
88	v	Warren⁶ b. 15 Oct. 1805.	
	vi	Esther⁶ b. 29 Sept. 1807.	
	vii	Lucy-Fish⁶ b. 31 Jan. 1813 ; d. unm. 26 Oct. 1828.	

He d. 24 Aug. 1833; his widow d. 6 Jan. 1842.

50. Cyrus[5] Ayres of Brookfield, m. Betsy Adams, 10 April, 1800, and had

89
i Mary[6] b. 18 Feb. 1801.
ii Eliza[6] b. 3 Dec. 1802; d. 15 Dec. 1804.
iii Adeline[6] b. 8 Aug. 1804; m. Moses Greenwood.
iv Eliza[6] b. 6 April, 1806; m. —— Loring.
v William-Adams[6] b. 12 Sept. 1807.
vi Cyrus[6] b. 24 Sept. 1809; living unm.
vii Fanny-Hale[6] b. 29 Nov. 1813; m. Reuben Stowe.
viii Sally-Wait[6] b. 27 Feb. 1815; d. 18 July, 1820.
ix Sophronia-Rice[6] b. 28 Feb. 1817; m. 1. Emerson Kent. 2. Cheney Hatch.
x Charlotte[6] b. 28 April, 1819; m. Francis Richardson.

His wife d. 8 Nov. 1822; and he d. 19 Nov. 1822.

51. John[5] Ayres of Brookfield and Boston, m. at Truro, Rebecca Lombard, 15 Nov. 1803, and had

90
i Lovice[6] b. 3 Aug. 1805; born at Provincetown, m. Charles O. Whitmore, and d. 27 Sept. 1848, leaving five children.
ii John[6] b. 26 July, 1807; b. at Truro.
iii Matilda[6] b. 18 Nov. 1809; d. 22 Aug. 1811.
iv Matilda[6] b. 9 June, 1813; d. 28 Aug. 1814.
v Mary-Nickerson[6] b. 2 July, 1817; b. at Duxbury.
vi Rebecca-Olive[6] b. 9 Nov. 1819; b. at Boston.
vii Harriet-Fish[6] b. 4 Dec. 1825; d. 14 March, 1826.

He d. 22 Aug. 1830, at Boston, and his widow d. 26 Dec. 1852, aged 69.

52. Stephen⁵ Ayres of Fairfield, Herkimer co. N. Y., m. Roxy Snow, in 1795, and had

91	i William⁶ b.	1797.
	ii Clara⁶ b.	1800; m. Asahel Barnes of Colosse, Oswego co., N. Y.
92	iii Alexander⁶ b.	1802.
93	iv Hiram⁶ b.	1803.
	v Mary⁶ b.	1806; m. Ackland Salisbury of Norway, Herkimer co.
94	vi Jason⁶ b.	1808.
	vii Angeline⁶ b.	1811; m. Nath'l Henderson of Himrod's. Yates co. N. Y.
	viii Laura⁶ b.	1814; d. unm. about 1842.
	ix Persis⁶ b.	1818; d. unm. about 1838.

He d. in 1850; his widow d. in 1853.

53. Henry⁵ Ayres of Manheim, N. Y. and Allensville, Switzerland co. Ind., m. Abigail Bean, and had

95	i Alexander⁶ b.	1811.
	ii Adeline⁶ b.	1813; m. George Platt.
96	iii Horace-M.⁶ b.	1815.
	iv Maria⁶ b.	1818; m. James R. Fisher.
	v Charles⁶ b.	1820; d. unm. in 1838.
	vi Julia⁶ b.	1822; m. —— Edwards.
	vii Henry⁶ b.	1825; m. and had one child.
	viii Roxanna⁶ b.	1828; m. Stephen Peabody.
	ix Edwin⁶ b.	1833; m. lives at Champaign, Ill.

He d. in 1857 or 8, aged 81.

54. Elijah⁵ Ayres m. 1st, Louisa Stone of Manheim, Herkimer co. N. Y., and had

	i John⁶ b.	1813; d. same year.

His wife d. in 1814, and in 1817 he m. 2d, Emma Brayton, and had

    ii Eliza⁵ b.   1818; d.
    iii Mary⁵ b.   1820; m. D. B. Jones, of Little Falls, Herkimer co.
    iv Susan⁵ b.   1821; d.

His wife d. about 1840, and he moved to Trenton, Oneida co. N. Y., where he d. in 1847.

55. Silvanus⁴ Ayres of Manheim, Herkimer co. N. Y., m. Anna Bean, in 1815, and had

    i Emeline⁵ b.   1816; d.   1817.
97   ii Ebenezer⁵ b.   1817; m. Lucy T. Connelly, and has no children.
    iii Hannah⁵ b.   1819; m. O. B. Somerset, of Mic. . . .
    iv Olive⁵ b.   1820; m. A. F. Murphy, of Dixon, Il.
    v Charlotte⁵ b.   1822; m. Leonard Pratt, of Princeton, Mille Lac co. Minn.
    vi Fanny⁵ b.   1824; u. m.
    vii Anna⁵ b.   1825; d. unm. 1843.
    viii John-Silvanus⁵ b.   1831; d. unm. 1846.
98   ix Jason-C.⁵ b.   1835.

He d. near Fort Wayne, Ind., in 1840; his widow lives with her son Jason C. Ayres.

56. Daniel⁴ Ayres of St. Johnsville, Montgomery co. N. Y., m. 1st, Damaris Voorhees, 6 May, 1810, and had

99   i Daniel-Douglas⁵ b. 19 Aug. 1812.
    ii William-T.⁵ b.   1814; d. 24 June, 1814
    iii Mary-A.⁵ b. 3 Dec. 1815; m. Dr. Carroll.

His wife d. 18 Oct. 1817, and he m. 2d, Electa Lamb, 3 May, 1819, and had

	iv	James⁶ b. 19 Jan. 1820;	d. 20 May, 1820.
100	v	James-S.⁶ b. 13 May, 1821.	
101	vi	Alexander-Hamilton⁶ b. 24 March, 1823.	
102	vii	Romeyn-Beck⁶ b. 20 Dec. 1825.	
	viii	John-Lamb⁶ b. 24 March, 1828.	d. 16 May, 1833.
	ix	Darwin-E.⁴ b. 7 Meh, 1829;	d. 16 May, 1831.
103	x	Darwin⁶ }	
	xi	Irwin⁶ } b. 20 Mch, 1832.	
	xii	Richard-S.⁶ b. 10 Mch, 1834;	d. 24 Oct. 1834.
	xiii	Charles-S.⁶ b. 4 Jan. 1836.	

His wife dying 26 Feb. 1842, he m. 3rd, Margaret Freeman, 20 Sept. 1842. He d. 25 May, 1853.

57. John⁵ Ayres of Granby, m. Ruth Smith, and had

i	Ezra⁶ b. 5 Sept. 1771 ;	
ii	Irene⁶ b. 9 Sept. 1773 ;	d. Feb. 1843.
iii	Sarah⁶ b. 7 Dec. 1775.	
iv	Electa⁶ b. 4 April, 1778 ;	d. 15 Jan. 1849.
v	Enos⁶ b. 20 Sept. 1780.	
vi	Elihu⁶ b. 28 Jan. 1783 ;	d. Dec. 1801.
vii	Rhoda⁶ b. 19 Jan. 1785 ;	d. 29 March, 1855.
viii	Risa⁶ b. 20 June, 1786 ;	d. 29 March, 1817.
ix	Ruth⁶ b. 23 Feb. 1788	
x	Persis⁶ b. 19 Oct. 1790.	
xi	Sina⁶ b. 7 Jan. 1795.	

He d. 26 Jan. 1817.

58. Aaron³ Ayres of Granby, m. 1st, Lois Moody, 9 Jan. 1772, and had

i	Pliny⁶ b. 23 Dec. 1772 ;	d. 7 June, 1773.
ii	Pliny⁶ b. 23 Dec. 1775 ;	m. but d. s. p.
iii	Susannah⁶ b. 26 June, 1778 ;	m. Phinehas South.
iv	Samuel⁶ b. 8 July, 1780 ;	d. unm.
v	Roxana⁶ b. 1 Jan. 1783 ;	m. Eldin Clark.
vi	Quartus⁶ b. 3 Oct. 1785 ;	d. 5 Sept. 1828.
104 vii	Rodney⁶ b. 9 May, 1788.	

His first wife d. 26 Sept. 1789, and he m. 2d, Mary Hitchcock, 10 June, 1790, and had

105 viii	Calvin⁶ b. 4 Jan. 1791.	
ix	Lois⁶ b. 14 July, 1795 ;	m. William Belden.
x	Polly⁶ b. 22 Sept. 1797 ;	m. Augustus Clark.
xi	Emilia⁶ b. 12 Dec. 1800.	

He d. 9 April, 1813, and his widow (b. 9 Oct. 1761) d. 22 June, 1830.

59. Eleazer³ Ayres of Granby, m. Sybil, dau. of Israel Clark, and had

i	Chester⁶ b. 15 Nov. 1780 ;	d. 16 June, 1783.
ii	Elijah⁶ b. 6 June, 1782 ;	d. 11 Sept. 1784.
iii	Sybil⁶ b. 18 Dec. 1783 ;	d. 19 June, 1795.
106 iv	Chester⁶ b. 18 Sept. 1785.	
v	Dorcas⁶ b. 30 April, 1787 ;	m. Rev. David Pease.
vi	Elijah⁶ b. 6 March, 1789 ;	d. 2 May, 1797.
vii	Hannah⁶ b. 22 April, 1791 ;	d. 5 Sept. 1795.
107 viii	Edward⁶ b. 9 March, 1793.	

He d. 3 March, 1832; his wife d. 23 Feb. 1796, aged 38.

[Nos. 60, 61, and 62 are untraced.]

63. Moses[5] **Ayres** of Brookfield and of Barnard, Vt., m. Lucy Cutting, 1 Jan. 1777, and had

    i Lucy[6] b. 23 Sept. 1777.
    ii Dolly[6] b. 29 July, 1779 ;   d. 19 Nov. 1844.
    iii John[6] b. 16 Sept. 1781.
    iv James[6] b. 27 Sept. 1783 ;   d. unm.
    v Josiah[6] b. 27 Oct. 1785 ;   d. 11 July, 1786.
    vi Isaac[6] b. 27 May, 1787 ;   d. unm.
    vii Josiah[6] b. 13 Sept. 1789.
    viii Lydia[6] b. 21 May, 1792.

64. Eli[5] **Ayres** of Brookfield, m. Sally Crawford, of Oakham, (pub. 5 April, 1790,) and had

    i Patty[6] b. 24 April, 1791.
    ii Betsey[6] } b. 29 Oct. 1792.
    iii Nancy[6] }
    iv Rachel[6] b. 5 Aug. 1794.
    v Adam[6] b. 28 July, 1796.
    vi Sally[6] b. 21 Aug. 1798.

65. Jesse[5] **Ayres** of Brookfield, m. Abigail Tyler, (pub. 7 Sept. 1783,) and had

    i Hannah[6] b. 7 Feb. 1784.
    ii Sally[6] b. 26 Jan. 1786.

66. Jude[5] **Ayres** of Brookfield, m. Sally Babbitt, (pub. 25 Dec. 1786,) and had

    i Lucinda.[6]
    ii Persis.[6]
    iii Celia.[6]

He d. 5 Nov. 1815; his widow d. 4 March, 1838.

67. Increase[5] Ayres of Brookfield, m. at Leominster, 19 Nov. 1797, Jemima Houghton, and had

	i	Harriet[6] b. 11 Dec. 1798;	m. Billings Swan.
	ii	Amos[6] b. 4 April, 1800;	d. 24 Aug. 1855.
108	iii	Moses[6] b. 17 Jan. 1802.	
	iv	Melicent[6] b. 3 Oct. 1804;	d. 15 Sept. 1806.
	v	Clarissa[6] b. 23 Jan. 1807;	d. 6 Sept. 1859.
	vi	Dolly-Houghton[6] b. Dec. 1809; d. 19 Nov. 1811.	
109	vii	James-Converse[6] b. 7 Feb. 1812.	

He d. 13 May, 1840; his widow d. 6 Sept. 1850.

68. Capt. William[5] Ayres 3d of Brookfield, m. Freelove Jenks, 24 Oct. 1788, and had

110	i	William[6] b. 10 Jan. 1790.	
	ii	Freelove[6] b. 21 Sept. 1791; m. Charles Henshaw, and d. 26 April, 1816.	
	iii	Lucy[6] b. 7 Jan. 1794;	d. 10 Sept. 1796.
111	iv	Jonathan-Jenks[6] b. 28 March, 1797.	
	v	Lucy-Harrington[6] b. 23 Feb. 1800;	m. —— Cary.
	vi	Windsor[6] b. 24 May, 1803;	d. 14 May, 1807.
112	vii	Horace[6] b. 7 April, 1806;	
	viii	Samuel-Windsor[6] b. 26 Mar. 1809;	d. 10 Aug. 1811.

He d. 9 Jan. 1835; his widow d. 6 Sept. 1837.

69. Buenos[5] Ayres of Brookfield, m. Rachel Hamilton, (pub. 10 March, 1789,) and had

70. Joseph[5] Ayres of Brookfield, m. 13 Dec. 1795, Anna Dexter, and had

71. Benjamin[5] Ayres of Brookfield.

SIXTH GENERATION.

72. William-Henry⁶ Ayres of Brookfield, m. Sarah Hill, 16 April, 1838, and had

    i John-Winslow⁷ b. 14 Oct. 1840; living unm.
    ii Adaliza-Nye⁷ b 25 Jan. 1843.
    iii Susie-Ella⁷ b. 17 Oct. 1849 ; d. 3 Oct. 1851.
    iv Ella-Isabelle⁷ b. 2 Nov. 1851.

73. Perley⁶ Ayres of Oakham, Mass., m. 1st, Aug. 1, 1826, Grace Tidd, who d. 21 Jan. 1838. They had one son, b. 2 Dec. 1827, who d. soon. They then adopted Adeline U. Stearns, of Spencer, whose name was changed to A. U. Ayres by Act of the Legislature.

    i Adeline-U⁷   : m. Wm. A. Spear.

He m. 2d, Harriet W. Knight, 29 Aug. 1838, and had

    ii Sarah-Grace⁷ b. 14 July, 1839 ; m. George Avery.
    iii Louisa-A.⁷ b. 30 Jan. 1841.
    iv Hiram⁷ b. 29 Sept. 1842 ;   d. 27 Aug. 1859.
    v Charles-P.⁷ b. 30 Apr. 1844 ; d. 19 April, 1846.
    vi Eunice-H.⁷ b. 25 Dec. 1845 ;
    vii Catharine-A.⁷ b. 22 Oct. 1847 ; m. Edward L. Soper.

74. Isaac⁶ Ayres of Petersham, Mass., m. Charlotte Foster, 1 Sept. 1827, and had

    i Edwin⁷ b. 16 July, 1828.
    ii Miranda⁷ b. 21 Jan. 1830 ;   d. 22 June, 1833.
    iii Martha⁷ b. 16 June, 1832.
    iv George⁷ b. 26 Aug. 1833 ;   m. Sarah Spooner, 29 Nov. 1860.
    v Juliette⁷ } b 21 May, 1839 ;
    vi Maryette⁷ }   d. 8 Oct. 1839.

75. Elias⁴ Ayres of New Braintree, m. 1st, Asenath Cunningham, 1825, and had

  i Nancy-B.⁵ b. 19 June, 1826 ; m. C. L. Babbitt.
  ii Hiram⁵ b. 28 Oct. 1828 ; d. unm. in Cal. 22 Feb. 1867.
  iii Samuel⁵ b. 9 Aug. 1831 ; d. 27 Aug. 1833.
  iv Jane-H.⁵ b. 25 Aug. 1833 ; m. Albert Thurber.
  v Samuel⁵ b. 10 Nov. 1836 ; d. 11 July, 1857.
  vi Henry⁵ b. 6 May, 1838 ; m. Elvira Hawkes, 4 April,
               1866.
  vii William⁵ b. 23 Aug. 1841.
  viii Joseph⁵ b. 25 July, 1843 ; d. young.

His wife dying July, 1843, he m. 2d, Anne (Childs) widow of —— Hawkes, and had

  ix Martha⁵ b. 13 Feb. 1845.
  x Ellen-E.⁵
  xi Emma-V.⁵
  xii James-T.⁵
  xiii Daniel-Webster.⁵

He removed to Virginia in 1846, and his four youngest children were born there. He d. 25 March, 1869.

76. John⁶ Ayres of New Braintree, m. Diadamia Whipple, 30 June, 1818, and had

  i Elizabeth-Hassard⁵ b. 15 June, 1819 ; m. Benj. Upton.
  ii Sarah-E.⁵ b. 8 Nov. 1820 ; m. James Packard.
  iii John-Whipple⁵ b. 18 March,
    1822 ;   m. —— Packard, and lives
               in Milwaukie.
  iv Moses-Oliver⁵ b. 21 July, 1826 ; m. —— Farnham.
  v Diadamia⁵ b. 4 April, 1829 ; d. 4 May, 1855.
  vi Mary-Anne⁵ b. 12 March, 1833 ; m. Lucian Hill.
  vii Catharine-M.⁵ b. 29 April, 1837.

77. Anson⁴ Ayres.
    (Record not received.)

78. Tilley⁶ Ayres of   , m. Alvira
Cochrane, 20 March, 1824, and had

    i   Charlotte-S.⁷ b. 18 Nov. 1826 ;   m. Silas Cochrane.
   ii   Samantha-L.⁷ b. 17 Aug. 1828 ; d. 9 March, 1850.
  iii   Maria-E.⁷ b. 18 Aug. 1832 ;   d. 9 Aug. 1851.
  iv   Cynthia-E.⁷ b. 25 Jan. 1835 ;   d 19 April, 1850.
   v   Silas-C.⁷ b. 7 June, 1837 ;   d. 18 Nov. 1838.
  vi   Helen⁷ b. 11 Nov. 1842.
  vii   Ella⁷ b. 23 July, 1846.

79. Hiram⁶ Ayres of Duane, Vt., m. Philinda
Bigelow, 10 March, 1825, and had

    i   Alma⁷ b. 29 Oct. 1826 ;   d. 25 Aug. 1828.
   ii   Thirza⁷ b. 9 April, 1829 ;   m. Wiear L. Rowell.
  iii   Alma⁷ b. 22 Jan. 1831 :   m. E. W. Steenberg.
* iv   William-I.⁷ b. 22 Feb. 1833.
   v   Mary-I.⁷ b. 29 Aug. 1835 ;   m. Henry R. Thomson.
  vi   Louisa⁷ b. 1 Jan. 1838 :   m. Buell Foote.
  vii   Hiram⁷ b. 24 May, 1841.
 viii   Adeline⁷ b. 19 Jan. 1844 :   d. 6 Feb. 1847.
  ix   Eveline⁷ b. 7 July, 1846 ;   d. 29 Oct. 1862.

80. Eli⁶ Ayres of Royalton, Vt., m. Melinda
Peck, 7 Sept. 1825, and had

    i   Sidney K.⁷ b. 9 April, 1826 : m. Annis Clement.
   ii   Eliza⁷ b. 22 Sept. 1827 ;   m. John Hanson.
† iii   Anson⁷ b. 22 Sept. 1829.
  iv   Sarah-A.⁷ b. 9 Sept. 1831 ;   m. William Miller.
   v   Esther-M.⁷ b. 20 June, 1835 : d. 28 Feb. 1865.
  vi   Roxy-L.⁷ b. 1 Nov. 1837 ;   m. John Bramley.
  vii   Olive-K.⁷ b. 1 July, 1839 :   m. Charles Randall.
 viii   Harriet⁷ b. 20 Feb. 1842 ;   m. Orin Church.
  ix   Mary-I.⁷ b. 26 Feb. 1845 ;   m. Truman Rice.
   x   Susan⁷ b. 26 April, 1847 ;   m. Amasa Fuller.
  xi   Libbie⁷ b. 10 May, 1849 ;   d. 11 Oct. 1865.

---

* William-I.⁷ Ayres m. 14 Feb. 1860, Frances Merrill, and had Herbert-E.⁸ b. 14 Jan. 1861 ; Eva-E.⁸ b. 19 Feb. 1863 ; Frances-G.⁸ b. 18 April, 1866 ; William-Watson⁸ b. 20 June, 1869.

† Anson⁷ Ayres m. Mary Fuller, 1 Feb. 1855, and had Robert-P.⁸ b. 1 Dec. 1855 ; Clara-R.⁸ b. 18 July, 1857 ; Walter-H.⁸ b. 3 Dec. 1861 ; Anna-M.⁸ b. 10 April, 1864 ; Jennie-F.⁸ b. 31 Aug. 1866.

81. Joseph⁶ Ayres of Peru, N. Y., m. Mary Blodgett, 31 July, 1836, and had

i Almira⁷ b. 21 Jan. 1837 ;   m. John French.
ⁱ ii Nahum-Henry⁷ b. 25 March, 1840.
iii Mary-Jane⁷ } b. 24 Feb. 1846; d. 10 April, 1853.
iv Martha-Anne⁷ }
v Joseph-Franklin⁷ b. 24 Jan. 1846.
vi Emma-Adelaide⁷ b. 6 May, 1847.

82. Francis⁶ Ayres of   m. Catharine M. Gully, June, 1830, and had

i Almira⁷ b. 26 Aug. 1831 ;   d.   1858.
† ii Watson-M.⁷ b. 11 May, 1833.
iii Eleanor-M.⁷ b. 27 Feb. 1835; m. John H. Sprague.
iv Wealthy⁷ b. 7 May, 1837 ;   m. L. W. Hazeltine.
v Adeline⁷ b. 14 April, 1839.
vi Diana⁷ b. 1 Oct. 1841 ;   m. H. B. Dodge.
vii Sarah-J.⁷ b. 26 Aug. 1843 ; m. W. Hurlburt.
viii Alzina⁷ b. 25 March, 1845 ; m. N. H. Ayres, her cousin.

83. Jefferson⁶ Ayres of   m. Esther M. Miller, 1 March, 1832, and had

i Alphan⁷ b. 4 July, 1833 ;   m. Susan Leonard.
‡ ii Tyler⁷ b. 20 April, 1837.

84. Dudley-J.⁶ Ayres of   m. 1st. Elizabeth Clough, Dec. 1837, and had

§ i David-C.⁷ b. 6 Nov. 1841
ii Wallace⁷ b. 9 Feb. 1853.

---

* Nahum-Henry⁷ Ayres m. Alzina, dau. of Francis Ayres, (No. 82,) and had a daughter born 16 Sept. 1867, d. Feb. 1868.

† Rev. Watson M.⁷ Ayres m. 1 Dec. 1864, Ethaline H. Ainsworth, and had Clara-Grace⁸ b. 6 March, 1868 ; Charles-Francis⁸ b. 3 March, 1869.

‡ Tyler⁷ Ayres m. 1 March, 1859, Mary Fowler, and had Flora-M.⁸ b. 18 Jan. 1860; Charles-A.⁸ b. 26 Sept. 1861; Herbert-O.⁸ b. 17 May, 1867.

§ David-C.⁷ Ayres m. Catharine Moors, and had Samuel-J.⁸ b. April, 1867.

His wife d. Aug. 1860, and he m. 2d, May, 1861, Cornelia C. Signor, and had

    iii Almira-E.[7] b. 25 Jan. 1864.

85. **Marshall**[6] **Ayres** of Griggsville, m. Hannah Lombard, 21 Jan. 1834, and had

    * i Marshall[7] b. 20 Feb. 1839.
    ii Charles[7] b. 16 Sept. 1849 ; d. 27 July, 1851.

86. **Dana**[6] **Ayres** of   m. Alice Cleveland, and had

    i Delia[7]   ; m. Jas. Carpenter.
    ii Charles[7]

87. **Baxter**[6] **Ayres** of   m. Mary L. Gilbert, April, 1821, and had

    i Mary-J.[7]
    Lucy-Fish.[7]

88. **Warren**[6] **Ayres** of Worcester, m. Rachel S. Denny, 1 Dec. 1831, and had

    i Sarah-J[7]
    ii Charles-S.[7]
    iii Martha-D.[7]
    iv Anne-E.[7]
    v Carrie-F.[7]   d. 22 July, 1869.
    vi Ellen-M.[7]
    vii George-W.[7]   d. 18 Jan. 1845.

89. **William-Adams**[6] **Ayres** of Worcester, m. Caroline Hooker.

---

* Marshall[7] Ayres, jr. m. Louise-A. Sanderson, of Galesburg, Ill., 11 June, 1868, and had Mary-Louise * b. 5 July, 1869.

90. John[a] **Ayres** of Boston, m. Elizabeth Pope, 13 Aug. 1835, and had

    i Helen-Frances[7] b. 3 July, 1836.
    ii Alice-Cleveland[7] b. 17 May, 1838.
    iii Elizabeth[7] b. 26 May, 1840.
    iv Mary-Adeline[7] b. 16 April, 1844.

91. William[6] **Ayres** of Fairfield and Bassie, St. Lawrence co. N. Y., m. Jemima Potter, in 1818, and had

    i Matilda[7] b.   1819 ; m. Abner Breese, 1848.
    ii Albert[7] b.   1820 ; lives at Harrisville, St. Lawrence co.
    iii Roxana[7] b.   1822 ; m. Thomas Hurlburt, 1857.
    iv Stephen[7] b.   1824 ; m. Samantha Breese ; lives at Gouverneur, St. Lawrence co.
    v Alden[7] b.   1830 ; d. unm. 1835.
    vi William-H.[7] b.   1835 ; d. unm. 1856.
    vii Watts[7] b.   1837.

He d. in 1850.

92. Alexander[6] **Ayres** of Gouverneur, St. Lawrence co. N. Y., m.   and had

    i Stephen[7] b.   ; lives at Gloversville, Fulton co. N. Y.
    ii Adelisa[7] b.   :
    iii Marshall[7] b.   :
    iv Cyrus[7] b.   :
    v Mary[7] b.   ; m. Orlando Baldwin.

93. Hiram[6] **Ayres** of Fairfield, Herkimer co. N. Y., m. Electa Tuttle in 1837, and had

    i Romeyn-B[7] b.   1838.
    ii Maria[7] b.
    iii Harriet[7] b.   1844 ; m. Laurence La Rue.

94. Jason⁶ Ayres, of Poland, Herkimer co.
N. Y., m. Julia Ellison, and has no children.

95. Alexander⁶ Ayres of St. Johnsville and
Fort Plain, Montgomery co., N. Y., m. Harriet Farr,
and had

i Sarah-Helen⁷ b.	1838 ; d.	
ii Walter⁷ b.	1839 ; m. Flora Connor.	
iii Douglas⁷ b.	1842.	
iv Albert⁷ b.	1845.	
v Harriet⁷ b.	1847.	
vi Alexander⁷ b.	1850.	
vii Helen-M.⁷ b.	1853.	

96. Horace M.⁶ Ayres of Allensville, Switzer-
land co. Ind., m. Eliza Humphrey, and had

i Romeyne-B.⁷ b.   1840 ; killed in the war, 20 Jan. 1864.
ii Helen-M.⁷ b. 20 Jan. 1843 ; d. unm. 1863.
iii Adeline⁷ b. 9 Oct. 1848 ;   d. 1849.
iv Charles-S.⁷ b. 21 Dec. 1849.
v Henry-B.⁷ b. 11 Nov. 1853.
vi James-W.⁷ b. 26 Dec. 1855.
vii Elizabeth⁷ b. 30 Dec. 1857.

97. Ebenezer⁶ Ayres of Cottage Grove, Wash-
ington co. Minn., m. Lucy T. Connolly in 1846, and
has no children.

98. Jason C.⁶ Ayres of Dixon, Lee co. Ill., m.
Lavinia Crawford in 1860, and had

i Anna⁷

99. Daniel-Douglas Ayres m. Mary May, of Chillicothe, O., and had

    i Mary b.   ; m. C. H.

    ii Ella b.

100. James-S. Ayres of Kalamazoo, Mich., m. Amelia Andrus in 1846, and had

    i Mary b.   1848.
    ii Andrus b.   1851.
    iii Nelson b   1856.

101. Alexander-Hamilton Ayres of Fort Plain, Montgomery co. N. Y., m. 1st, Christiana L. Mabee, 15 Jan. 1856, who d. in the same year. He m. 2d, Emily G. Mabee, sister of his first wife, 11 Aug. 1857, and had

    i Irwin-Mabee b. 26 Nov. 1859; d.   1860.
    ii Mabee b. 6 May, 1866.
    iii Mary b 11 May, 1869.

102. Romeyn-Beck Ayres Major General, U. S. A., m. —— daughter of Col. Greenleaf Dearborn, and had

    i Romeyn-D. b. 6 Jan. 1851; d.   1854.
    ii Charles-G. b. 26 Feb. 1854.
    iii Mary-B b 9 July, 1856.
    iv Annie-S b 23 Nov. 1857; d.
    v Emily-D. b. 2 April, 1860.
    vi Henry-D b. 21 Sept. 1861.
    vii George-H. b. 23 Aug. 1865.

103. Darwin[6] **Ayres** m. Attelia Holt, ———
and had

> i Mary[7] b.   1867.

104. Rodney[6] **Ayres** m. Elizabeth Nash, 22
Aug. 1819, and had

> i S.-Augusta[7] b. 12 Aug. 1820 ; m. Emory Stebbins.
> ii Lois-Moody[7] b. 24 June, 1822.
> iii Henry[7] b. 23 Dec. 1824 ; d.
> iv William[7] b. 29 Feb. 1828.
> v Elizabeth[7] b. 20 April, 1833 ; d.
> vi Susan-Roxana[7] b. 13 June, 1836 ; d.

His wife d. 11 Dec. 1838, and he m. 2d, his cousin
Rhoda Felton Ayres, (dau. of John, 57,) 27 Nov.
1844; she d. 29 March, 1855, and he d. 19 June, 1867.

105. Calvin[6] **Ayres** m. Sarah Shaw, 11 April,
1817, and had

> * i Samuel[7] b. 3 June, 1818.
> † ii Pliny-W.[7] b. 11 April, 1820.

106. Chester[6] **Ayres** m. Lois Preston, 2 Oct.
1807, and had

> i Sybil[7] b. 7 March, 1808 ;   m. Addison Gridley.
> ii Maria[7] b. 16 July, 1810;   d. 12 Aug. 1813.
> iii Clarissa[7] b. 11 April, 1813 ; d. 22 Oct. 1834.

---

* Samuel[7] Ayres, m. Emeline Rice, and had Sarah,[8] (dead) Charles-R.,[8]
Samuel-E.,[8] (d. 19 Sept. 1849,) Ella-A.,[8] and Samuel-A.[8] His wife d. 5
March, 1860, and he m. 2d, Sarah-A. Fuller.

† Pliny-Washington[7] Ayres, m. Mary Hollister, and had Julia,[8] David,[8]
Henry,[8] and Emilia.[8] He lives in McGrawville, N. Y.

iv Louisa⁷ b. 7 Sept. 1815 ;   m. Dr. Wm. Bassett
v Sophia⁷ b. 3 May, 1818 ;   d. 22 Dec. 1878.
• vi Langdon⁷ b. 7 Nov. 1820.
vii Marie-Josephine⁷ b. 19 Nov.
          1823 ;   m. William W. Love
viii Harriet L.⁷ b. 27 Jan. 1838 ; d. 31 Jan. 1846.

He d. 10 March, 1858; his widow d. 3 Jan. 1869,
aged 83 years.

107. Edward⁶ Ayres m. Rachel Kent, 25 May, 1816, and had

+ i Rowland⁷ b. 1 May, 1817.
ii Samuel-Emilius⁷ b. 8 Feb. 1819 ; d. 2 Oct. 1819.
iii Emilius⁷ b. 9 June, 1820.
iv Marion-Jemima⁷ b. 24 Sept. 1821 ; d. 27 May, 1857.
v Dorcas-Laurentia⁷ b. 8 March, 1823 ; d. 16 March, 1824.
vi Juliet⁷ b. 26 Dec. 1824 ; m. George N. Smith.
vii Amoret⁷ b. 26 Aug. 1826 ; m. Chas. Smith.
viii Edward-Romaine⁷ b. 6 Aug. 1828 ; d. Feb. 1848.
ix Everard⁷ b. 31 Aug. 1830.
x David-Cornelius⁷ b. 27 Dec. 1832.

His wife d. 30 Oct. 1830; he d. 11 May, 1842.

108. Moses⁶ Ayres of N. Brookfield m. Sophronia Waite, June, 1827, and had

i Harriet-Swan⁷ b.   ; d.   aged 19.
ii Windsor⁷ b.   ; m. and lives in Worcester.
iii Samuel-W.⁷ b.   ; d.   aged 22.
iv Charlotte-E.⁷ b.   ; d.   aged 3.

* Langdon⁷ Ayres, m. 21 Nov. 1844, Drusilla Perley, by whom, who d. 7 Feb. 1851. He m. 2d, 11 May, 1853, Sarah Elizabeth Perley, and had Fred⁸ b. 16 April, 1854; Frank L.⁸ b. 25 Feb. 1856; James C.⁸ b. 6 July, 1858, and Arthur S.⁸ b. 5 Sept. 1861.

† Rev. Rowland⁷ Ayres of Amherst, Mass., m. 1 Aug. 1848, Caroline Webster, and had Alice-Juliet⁸ b. 5 Aug. 1849; Edward-Webster⁸ b. 6 Aug. 1851; Edith-Jane⁸ b. 13 March, 1860; Grace⁸ b. 12 Sep. 1861, d. 2 Apr. 1862; and Agnes⁸ b. 4 April, 1863.

109. **James-Converse**[6] **Ayres** of N. Brookfield, m. Lauretta Ruggles, of Hardwick, 25 Dec. 1838, and had

    i Henry-Warren[7] b. 1 March, 1844.
    ii George-Houghton[7] b. 25 Oct. 1845 ; d. 25 Sept. 1850.
    iii John-Dwight[7] b. 9 Feb. 1848 ; d. 19 Sept. 1850.
    iv Lauretta-A.[7] b. 8 July, 1850 ; d. 2 May, 1865.
    v Emma-A.[7] b. 11 Oct. 1852.
    vi William-F.[7] b. 16 May, 1855 ; d. 1 Feb. 1861.

110. **William**[6] **Ayres** of Brookfield, m. Mercy Phillips, and had

    i William-Winsor[7] b.   ; m. Mrs. Jane Fishback of St. Louis, and had William-E.[8] of Wasington.

111. **Jonathan-Jenks**[6] **Ayres** of Brookfield, m. 12 Dec. 1839, Sophia Emery, of Ware, and had

    i Ella-Sophia[7] b. 16 Aug. 1848 ; d.   Oct. 1848.

112. **Horace**[6] **Ayres** of Worcester, m. 1st, Harriet Woodworth, and had besides one son and one daughter who died, a daughter married to M. Clarke, of Worcester. He m. 2d, Caroline, dau. of Otis Corbett, and had

    i Horace-C[7] b.   1848.

INDEX.

I N D E X .

SURNAMES OTHER THAN AYRES

www.ingramcontent.com/pod-product-compliance
Lightning Source LLC
Chambersburg PA
CBHW021635270326
41931CB00008B/1034